Original title:
Life: Not as Complicated as I Thought

Copyright © 2025 Creative Arts Management OÜ
All rights reserved.

Author: Christian Leclair
ISBN HARDBACK: 978-1-80566-039-2
ISBN PAPERBACK: 978-1-80566-334-8

Painting Days with Ease

Woke up today, what a thrill,
My socks don't match, but I'm chill.
Coffee spills, a little mess,
Is this chaos or just success?

Found a spoon instead of a fork,
My breakfast is now a fun quirk.
Eggs on the floor, oh what a sight,
Maybe it's art, I'll call it bright!

The plants in pots, they all seem fine,
Watered them once, they want more time.
Yet here I laugh, not feeling blue,
They thrive on chaos, just like you!

Walking in circles, that's my dance,
Tripped on the dog, but hey, that's chance.
Laughter echoes in my small space,
Each silly moment adds to my grace.

A Universe in a Grain of Sand

Once I thought, I'd need a map,
But joy is found in a brief nap.
Stumbled on crumbs while I was lost,
Now I know the little things cost!

Found a sock beneath the bed,
"Where's the other?" spins in my head.
The cat's my guide, with her sly ways,
Together we wander through lazy days.

I tripped on a thought, it didn't hurt,
A wild idea where my dreams flirt.
In laughter, simplicity takes flight,
With every mishap, the world feels right.

So cheers to those grains, so divine,
For what's so small can brightly shine.
In quirks and laughs, we understand,
A universe waits in each grain of sand.

The Wisdom in the Waiting

In line for coffee, feeling bold,
A squirrel stole my muffin, so I'm told.
The barista laughs, I roll my eyes,
Patience is key, that's no surprise.

Time slips like sand through fingers tight,
Yet here I sit, it feels so right.
The universe chuckles, it's quite a show,
Teaching me lessons while I sip slow.

Puzzles with Missing Pieces

Each day's a puzzle, bits all askew,
Some pieces vanish, don't have a clue.
I've got corner bits, but the middle's a mess,
Laughter at chaos, that's my success.

I search for the edges, my cat takes a dive,
Knocking the box over, keeping hope alive.
Is that a rabbit or just a lost part?
Who needs the full picture? I've got a good heart!

Gentle Ripples on Still Water

A stone skips lightly, the pond is aglow,
Watch my thoughts scatter, to and fro.
"Is this deep water?" I ponder and laugh,
Maybe it's just my skinny five-year-old calf.

Nature's giggle echoes off the trees,
I shout back with glee, catching a breeze.
Life's simple joys float right on by,
Like ducks in a row—oh me, oh my!

A Tapestry of Small Wonders

Threads of laughter weave through my day,
A neighbor's laughter, a cat in a play.
I find joy in crumbs and in sidewalk cracks,
Watch out for the ants, in their tiny tracks.

Colors so vibrant, a butterfly flits,
Every small moment, the happiness fits.
We're all just stories stitched with care,
Finding joy in the mundane, everywhere!

Revelations in Gentle Moments

In a world where socks go missing,
I found joy in mismatched pairs.
Chasing dreams like a cat at dawn,
Turns out they were just light flares.

Coffee spills and laughter rise,
A dance with buttered toast,
Finding fun in daily chores,
Who knew I could laugh the most?

Amid the chaos, I dare to grin,
As excuses fall like autumn leaves.
I swear the universe just winks,
And nudges me with playful thieves.

So here I stand with open arms,
Embracing fails I once would frown.
The secret's clear — the rhythm's there,
Just join the song and spin around.

The Simplicity Beneath the Layers

I thought I needed grand designs,
But joy comes wrapped in tiny things.
Like finding treasures in the fridge,
A leftover bite, what bliss it brings.

Instructions often lead to mess,
A recipe gone wild and strange.
Yet popcorn's popping fills the air,
Salty smiles, who needs to change?

Pants two sizes too small, surprise!
They squeak when I sit, oh my!
Yet laughter bursts in stubborn seams,
A wardrobe choice, or just a lie?

Underneath the serious talk,
A whiff of humor lifts my mood.
It's in the little things I find,
The secret's simple, oh so good!

Whispers of the Ordinary

A traffic jam, a honk, a cheer,
I wave to strangers, smiles they send.
Each stoplight's a little dance,
Turns out, the fun will never end.

Grocery lists that go astray,
I end up with five different cheese.
Who knew I'd host a feast today,
With only crumbs and childhood dreams?

I thought I'd climb some mountain high,
When all I needed was a stroll.
The cracks in sidewalks tell their tales,
Of laughter shared and hearts made whole.

So here's to whispers, soft and sweet,
In every moment, big or small.
For joy is found in quirky bits,
And life's a party, after all!

Unraveling the Tangled Threads

A ball of yarn and a cat's delight,
What chaos springs from a tiny meow!
Each knot is reason to get a laugh,
Who needs perfection anyhow?

I tried to cook a gourmet feast,
But burnt the toast, it turned to stone.
Yet with a sprinkle of humor,
It transformed to a toaster throne!

To-do lists that never end,
Every box unchecked — what a scene!
I painted smiles on chores so grim,
Now I'm just a joyful machine.

So here's the truth in tangled threads,
Not all is as it seems to be.
With laughter lighting every path,
I find my way, forever free.

Sunsets in Slow Motion

The sun dips low, a lazy show,
Like socks that drift, in washer's flow.
Colors blend like mismatched shoes,
A canvas bright, with life's odd hues.

Birds chirp tunes in offbeat style,
Chasing light, they stop and smile.
The clouds parade, a fluffy crowd,
They're taking selfies, feeling proud.

Simplicity's Warm Embrace

A cup of tea, an unmade bed,
The cat just knocked my book instead.
Moments small, like crumbs on floors,
Bring giggles out from cozy stores.

My keys are lost, as always so,
They hide from me, a high-stakes show.
But laughter spills, like orange juice,
In chaos, there's a sweet excuse.

The Melody of Mundanity

The toaster pops, a morning song,
It plays a tune, and I hum along.
Chores and socks, a silly dance,
In every moment, give joy a chance.

The traffic's stuck, a game we play,
I sing my heart out on display.
With every honk, a new refrain,
Mundane, yet funny, all the same.

Light Through the Cracks

Sunlight spills through window seams,
Waking thoughts like scattered dreams.
Dust bunnies twirl in playful glee,
Who knew they'd join the party spree?

A crooked frame holds memories dear,
With all its flaws, it draws us near.
Perfectly broken, a charming find,
In quirky misfits, joy's defined.

The Canvas of Contentment

Brush strokes dance, colors collide,
A splotch of ketchup, side of fries.
Why worry 'bout the mess we make,
When every mistake breeds a new take?

A cat on the rug, it's all a show,
Chasing its tail, oh where'd it go?
We laugh at the chaos, embrace the fun,
With every misstep, feels like a home run.

Dinner was burned, smoke fills the air,
But laughter erupts, joy everywhere.
In the simplest things, a spark will ignite,
Frogs jump in puddles, what a delight!

So here's to the spills, the wild, the free,
Painting our dreams in chaos, you see?
With each joyous bump, we learn how to play,
Life's a funny canvas, in splendid disarray.

Murmurs of Unplanned Wonders

A trip to the store, I might just roam,
Forgotten the list, but hey, I'm home!
Chocolate and chips, what a surprise,
Came for milk, left with a sugary prize.

Unexpected rains turn skies into cheer,
Dancing in puddles, there's nothing to fear.
Umbrellas upside down, oh what a scene,
Laughing at how silly we all can be!

Plans laid out smooth, like butter on bread,
Yet curveballs are thrown, plans gone to bed.
But joy finds a way, through slip-ups and fun,
In moments unexpected, life's treasures are spun.

So shout to the wild, to the twists and turns,
Where laughter and whimsy play, and it burns!
Murmurs of wonder in every odd lane,
In chaos and glee, discover the gain.

The Sound of Peace in Chaos

Bells ringing loud, the kid's squeals burst,
The dog's gone nuts, it's absolute first!
But in this racket, a calm starts to bloom,
With giggles like chimes, there's always more room.

Fried eggs on the ceiling, who knew they could fly?
Panic? Nah! Just look at the pie!
Stay cool, breathe deep, embrace this sweet mess,
In chaos, we find out just how to bless.

Neighbors peek in, thinking we're nuts,
But laughter's a language that'll clear up the cuts.
So let the absurd wrap us in glee,
For joy in the noise is the best kind of spree.

So tiptoe through chaos, dance on the floor,
With every loud crash, let's open the door!
Find peace in the laughter, the stories we share,
In the sound of the storm, our hearts know no care.

Riddles of Simple Joy

A puzzle unsolved, with pieces so bright,
Turned upside down, but that feels just right.
With every wrong fit, we chuckle and grin,
In the dance of mistakes, we find joy within.

A shoe on the hand, what a strange hat,
Wearing mismatched socks, and we laugh at that!
For every odd choice, there's laughter galore,
In riddles of joy, we open each door.

Swinging so high, reaching for the skies,
With friends by my side, here's where the fun lies.
Spinning around like a tornado of cheer,
We swap tales of silliness, loud for all to hear.

So here's to the moments, bizarre and unclear,
Wrapped up within laughter, joy bubbling near.
In riddles most splendid, we learn to employ,
The charm of the simple, the magic of joy.

Epiphanies in the Dawn

The sun woke up, quite late today,
As birds forgot their lines to play.
I tripped on shoes that didn't fit,
And laughed at all the wobbly wit.

A coffee spill, a toast gone wrong,
I danced to tunes that did not belong.
The toast was burnt, the eggs were cold,
Yet somehow, joy was uncontrolled.

My neighbor's cat chased shadows near,
While I just marveled, filled with cheer.
A pile of socks, a missing shoe,
All seemed absurd; who knew it's true?

So here's to mornings wild and fleet,
Where chaos reigns and dreams compete.
Epiphanies in morning light,
As laughter bubbles, pure delight.

Reflections in a Teacup

I peered into my teacup bold,
And saw reflections, stories told.
A floating leaf, a dance of steam,
In every swirl, a silly dream.

The scone, it crumbled, made its mess,
A pastry fight? I must confess!
A spoon did wobble, tilted sly,
As crumbs did launch and higher fly.

Ironic thoughts in every sip,
As giggles grew from my teacup's lip.
The kettle whistled loud and clear,
And laughter echoed, drawing near.

So raise a cup and toast the day,
To little joys along the way.
In every splash, a giggling gale,
On this ridiculous, funny trail.

Laughter Beneath the Surface

In puddles deep, I stomped with glee,
As splashes danced around my knee.
Water shoes? Who needs that sight?
I'm just a fish in this delight!

My umbrella flipped, a silly fight,
An acrobat I am, in flight!
Each droplet seemed to laugh and sing,
My heart was light, my soul took wing.

Raindrops whispered secrets old,
As ducks quacked tales, both wise and bold.
I waved at clouds, my pal so great,
Together we conjured laughs of fate.

So here's to laughter's splashy wave,
To moments captured, bold and brave.
In rain-soaked joy, we find our grace,
A dance through puddles, a merry race.

A Symphony of Small Things

A pencil breaks, what a grand affair,
Yet laughter rises, filling the air.
A paper clip, who knew could fly?
Behold the wonders of the sly!

The clock ticked loud, with shaky hands,
It played a tune, like rock band bands.
With socks unmatched and coffee stains,
I wove a melody through my chains.

A sticky note, my friend so dear,
With doodles bright, it sparked a cheer.
Crayons melted, played a trick,
Turning into art, oh so quick!

In small things lies a joyful rhyme,
A symphony through space and time.
So laugh aloud at every call,
These moments lovely, small things tall.

The Space Between Breaths

I chased my thoughts like butterflies,
They danced away, oh how they fly.
I placed my feet on pillows soft,
And took a break, my worries scoff.

The toaster popped, I jumped about,
My breakfast saved, a joyful shout.
With coffee spilled across my shirt,
A splotch of brown, my fashion flirt.

I pondered over socks with stripes,
And tangled hair like dancing gripes.
Yet laughter bubbled deep inside,
As I embraced my silly stride.

So let the world be light and free,
With every breath, just let it be.
For in the chaos, find a grin,
The space between is where we win.

A Journey with Soft Footprints

I wandered through a field of grass,
Where daisies giggle as I pass.
With every step, a pop, a crack,
Like snacks being crushed with every track.

My sandals flew off like wild birds,
They never listened to my words.
I chased them down, a comical sight,
Two socks and shoes in silly flight.

I met a squirrel who wore a tie,
He chattered on as I walked by.
"Don't sweat the small stuff," he exclaimed,
I laughed so hard, my cheeks were framed.

And as I lounged beneath a tree,
The branches whispered tales to me.
With laughter echoing off the ground,
In soft footprints, joy is found.

Moments that Hold the Wind

I caught a breeze in a paper cup,
It tickled my nose and then blew up.
I ran with laughter, arms spread wide,
But every gust became my guide.

A kite flew high, a joyful dance,
I twirled around, lost in a trance.
But strings got tangled, oh such fun,
An acrobat's act, a jumbled run.

With giggles floating on the breeze,
I wished to sail the clouds with ease.
Yet tangled in a web of air,
I laughed so hard, I didn't care.

Each moment passed, a playful flirt,
In this wild ride, I found my worth.
For every whiff of wind I've had,
Gave back the giggles, oh so glad.

The Art of Just Being

In pajamas worn all day long,
I hummed a tune, an off-key song.
The clock played tricks, oh what a game,
Time sneezed loudly, it felt the same.

I poured my cereal, forgot the bowl,
Just used my hands, oh what a stroll.
With milk on my chin, a smile wide,
A breakfast mess, my joy couldn't hide.

I sat amid the cluttered space,
Found beauty in the silly trace.
With dishes piled like ancient hills,
I chuckled at my chaos spills.

For in each moment, small and spry,
I learned to laugh and just comply.
The art of being, light and free,
It's just as simple as can be.

The Simple Threads We Weave

In the mornings, I search for my sock,
But it's vanished, like a sneaky rock.
My keys play hide and seek with glee,
Oh where's the simplest part of me?

Coffee spills like a trusty friend,
Yet brings a smile that will not end.
I laugh at the mess, so brightly spread,
Guess messy mornings are just well-bred!

The cat decides to chase a fly,
I ponder why it won't ask me why.
We dance through chaos, you and I,
Finding joy in every little sigh.

With tangled threads behind my back,
I question if it's sense or snack.
In laughter's grip, I take a stand,
Embracing whims, as life's unplanned.

In the Garden of Moments

We plant our hopes like flowers bright,
But weeds of worry steal the light.
Yet in this garden, small and round,
A giggle blooms on shaky ground.

Bumblebees buzz, bring the cheer,
As I drop my sandwich – oh dear!
The ants march in with a party of snacks,
While I regret my relaxed lunch hacks.

The sun sneaks in through leafy green,
Tickling my nose, it's quite the scene.
Time hops around like a playful hare,
With each slight giggle, I toss my care.

Yet under the sun, I learn each day,
That joy grows close, come what may.
In moments spare, I take my cue,
To embrace the funny, enjoy the view.

Unfolding the Everyday

Waking up is like a grand surprise,
With pillow bumps and droopy eyes.
I stumble, fumble, find my way,
And laugh at the dawn of my misplay.

Breakfast sizzles, a pancake flip,
Only to witness it take a dip.
The dog looks on, with a panting grin,
As syrup drips, let the fun begin!

Running late, I wave goodbye,
To my favorite shirt, it's asking why.
Yet in the haste, I find my stride,
With laughter tucked deep, I'll abide.

In each mishap, a lesson shared,
The ridiculous moments, fully bared.
Unfolding joy in shades so bright,
The everyday blooms with pure delight.

Breezes Through the Open Window

A gentle breeze whispers sweet news,
While I search for the remote I lose.
Cushions fly like clouds in the air,
As I make decisions with utmost flair.

The snacks I hid just a few days back,
Have vanished, taken their own little track.
I chuckle as I find them in the drawer,
A treasure trove I can't ignore.

Birds chirp tunes from branches high,
As I awkwardly wave my hand to fly.
In silly dances, I find my beat,
Life's a jig—oh, it's oh-so-sweet!

With laughter wrapping around my whole,
Breezes carry me, free my soul.
In every twist, I relish this show,
Finding fun in all the woes.

Nature's Quiet Lessons

A leaf fell down, just like a dream,
It floated slowly, not a single scream.
The tree stood tall, a wise old chap,
Saying, 'Take it easy, maybe take a nap.'

The squirrel danced, quite full of nuts,
Chasing its tail, amidst all the ruts.
It laughed at worries, what a grand jest,
Said, 'Chill out, friend, it's all just a quest.'

Embracing the Now

The clock ticks on, but I just roll,
With pancakes flying, that's my goal.
I spill the syrup, it drips and twirls,
While my cat yawns, and the world unfurls.

A bird on a wire sings a tune,
While I munch crumbs beneath the moon.
I wave at the mailman, he's lost and confused,
But I smile wide, for I refuse to muse.

Sunlit Paths and Simple Choices

The sunbeams flicker, golden and bright,
I put on my socks, then laugh at the sight.
One's polka-dot, the other plain,
But who really cares? I won't complain.

I stroll along with ice cream in hand,
Savoring flavors, isn't life grand?
Do I walk left or do I veer right?
Oh well, there's a hot dog stand in sight!

The Subtle Beauty of Being

I tripped on my shoe, fell on the grass,
Laughed at myself through a silly class.
The flower giggled, oh what a mess,
It whispered softly, 'Just do your best.'

The ants marched on, a tiny parade,
Carrying crumbs in the sunlight's shade.
I joined the fun, with a silly cheer,
After all, who cares about the sneer?

Finding Ease in the Chaos

Juggling socks and cereal bowls,
A dance with toast, oh what controls!
Spilled coffee on my favorite shirt,
Laugh it off, I guess it won't hurt.

Plans so grand, they all fell through,
But who needs schedules when you can chew?
Chasing dreams on a sunset train,
Sometimes it's fun just to go insane.

A flat tire on a sunny morn,
Turns into tales that we adorn.
With each hiccup, a giggle's near,
In chaos, there's nothing to fear.

Picture this in your mind's embrace,
Silly dances in the strangest space.
The clutter here is simply divine,
I'll toast to messy days with wine!

The Art of Letting Go

Woke up late, what a sweet surprise,
Combs are missing, chaos underlies.
Rules bend and twist like silly rubber,
Laughing at things that make me stutter.

Can't find my keys, just what to do?
Must detangle this morning brew.
Jump in my car, and then I see,
It's good to leave, just let it be.

Spilled some milk, but that's okay,
It's just a mess, it won't betray.
A toast to crumbs and wild hair days,
Letting go brings out funny ways.

In the end, it's really a show,
Of all the blunders we learn to know.
Laughter echoes, bright and free,
In every stumble, joy's the key!

Whispers of the Ordinary

My plants are thirsty, oh dear child,
They call to me, their voices wild.
This laundry pile has grown a throne,
I might just leave it all alone.

Grocery lists that make no sense,
Apples in place of milk, suspense!
Oh, ice cream for dinner, who would've known?
In banality, the laughter's grown.

Traffic jams that feel like a race,
People talking in a silly space.
Waiting in line, I start to sway,
To the rhythms of a mundane day.

Yet every whisper of the routine,
Is a thread in fabric, pure and keen.
So I'll embrace the odd and grins,
Finding joy where the ordinary spins!

A Mosaic of Ordinary Days

Days stitched together, odd and bright,
With coffee spills and fuzzy fights.
Lost my shoe while on a stroll,
But look, it's just a tiny hole!

This quilt of time, both soft and neat,
Contains my moments, oh so sweet.
Pineapple on pizza, yes or no?
I'll eat it all, say it's a show!

Neighbors chatting through the fences,
In their quirks, life's best defenses.
A dance at dusk, random and free,
Each laugh a note in our melody.

So here's to days, stitched with care,
In the ordinary, we find flair.
Together they twinkle, a funny spree,
In a mosaic of you and me!

Wandering with an Open Heart

I strolled through the park with my shoe untied,
Watching squirrels think they're kings, nowhere to hide.
My coffee splashed down, a caffeinated mess,
Yet laughter bubbled up, I couldn't care less.

The sun played peek-a-boo among fluffy clouds,
I chuckled at ducks, queens of their crowds.
A breeze tickled my nose, oh what a delight,
I danced with my shadow, both feeling quite light.

A dog ran past wearing a bright yellow scarf,
I sighed, "If only I could inspire such a laugh!"
But here I am, a wanderer with heart,
Who knew simple joys could be a fine art?

As I journey through moments that come and go,
I've learned it's okay not to steal the show.
With open hearts, we can find our own way,
Oh, how silly and sweet is this beautiful play!

The Grace of Everyday Wisdom

Grandma once said, don't fret over crumbs,
While I sweep the floor to sweet-sounding drums.
I pondered her words, with a quizzical grin,
"Are you sure that's wisdom, or just a whim?"

I had a chat with my goldfish today,
It stared back, unimpressed by what I say.
I laughed at its bubbles, floating with grace,
Maybe fish don't judge, they just love the place.

The neighbor's cat naps on the warm sunny stoop,
I join in the fun, a delightful old troop.
With wisdom in purring and laughter in air,
We find that simplicity can be quite rare.

So let's toast to the truth hiding in plain sight,
To seize the day's giggles under the moonlight.
Every easy-going moment where we can find glee,
Reminds me there's wisdom in just being… me!

The Beauty in Clear Choices

I flipped a coin at breakfast today,
Pancakes or waffles? Such a tough play.
The coin rolled away, choosing for me,
Now I'm stuck in a syrupy spree!

Deciding to wear mismatched socks with glee,
Made my feet laugh, oh, how they felt free.
With each silly choice, I lightened my load,
Life's a bazaar with a whimsical code.

My friends planned a trip, from here to the moon,
A ridiculous thought, but my heart hummed a tune.
Yet here on my couch, Netflix and snacks,
I pondered adventures with chips at my backs.

So here's to the choices that make us all grin,
The small silly moments, let the fun begin!
With laughter and joy, we'll dance to the beat,
In the beauty of chaos, we'll find our retreat!

Embracing the Moments of Now

I tripped on my shoelace, but what a sweet fall,
Laughter erupted, I gave it my all.
A bird took a dive, or so I believed,
"Did it move like that just to see me deceived?"

With each little mishap, I spun on my toe,
The universe giggled, as if in the flow.
I spotted a rainbow—a spoon and a fork,
Okay, it was just my dreams talking, not cork.

But here in this moment, the chaos feels right,
With giggles and banter, a wonderful sight.
I'll ride each wave of the absurd and the wild,
For joy often dwells where we once were beguiled.

So let's pop the confetti, embrace what we've found,
In the moments of now, that joyful sound.
For life's all a giggle, a whimsical show,
If we laugh at ourselves, where else could we go?

Gentle Steps on Soft Ground

I stumbled on a blade of grass,
And wondered if I'd really pass.
With gentle steps, I took a chance,
To make my way, not miss the dance.

A rock appeared, it had a grin,
I asked it how it came to be in.
It chuckled back, said, "Just a stone,
Relax, my friend, you're not alone!"

The butterflies, they laughed with glee,
As I pretended to climb a tree.
I realized then, with a loud shout,
This world's a playground, there's no doubt!

So here I am, on soft ground still,
With absent worries, just for thrill.
A gentle sway, a giggly spin,
Who knew simplicity could begin?

Sunshine in Sips

I poured the sun into my cup,
And found it funny, that's what's up.
With every sip, I felt the spark,
And laughed at shadows chasing dark.

A lemon peel, a citrus twist,
I think I made a sunny mist.
The daisies joined, in swaying dance,
To celebrate my sipping chance.

The colors brightened, birds took flight,
As I toasted with delight tonight.
Every gulp, a giggle burst,
Who knew this joy could quench a thirst?

So raise your glass, find laughter's glow,
In every sip, let stories flow.
The sunshine's warmth, it fills the air,
With each sweet taste, we shed our care!

Revelry in Rustling Leaves

The leaves confided in the breeze,
With secrets shared and giggles, please.
They swirled around in wild delight,
A banquet of color, such a sight!

I joined the dance, with clumsy feet,
It felt like magic, so bittersweet.
Each rustle spoke of carefree times,
And whispered jokes in rhythmic rhymes.

The trees chuckled, their branches swayed,
I laughed along, no need to fade.
My worries flew, like birds on high,
As nature's comedy passed by.

So here I stand, among this cheer,
Where rustling leaves wipe every tear.
It's all a party, join the spree,
In nature's laughter, we're all free!

The Quietude of Happy Days

In quiet moments, joy cascades,
Like sunshine streaming through the shades.
I find a smile in simple things,
Like popcorn popping, laughter rings.

The clock ticks slow, a turtle's race,
I practice stillness, find my place.
With every second, giggles swell,
In solitude, where wonders dwell.

I count the clouds, like fluffy sheep,
Awakening dreams from cozy sleep.
A silly thought, I start to croon,
Dancing shadows beneath the moon.

On happy days, I let love reign,
Wrapped in quiet, I feel no pain.
With every breath, I feel so blessed,
In this calm chaos, I find my rest!

When Worries Fade to Background

Put on my shoes, they don't quite fit,
Chasing all my thoughts, they just won't sit.
The cat walks by with a teasing yawn,
Reminding me of better days to dawn.

I search for answers, I roam all around,
Turns out it's just the cat that I found.
With silly antics, they steal my sighs,
A tangled ball of yarn, oh my, oh my!

The mirror shows a funky hairdo,
But laughter bubbles, like morning dew.
Worries shrink like a puddle in sun,
Simplicity hides where we have our fun.

So chase the giggles, set free your heart,
Embrace the chaos, it's just the start.
For in the mess, there's clarity too,
A joyful twist to embrace the view.

Secrets in the Stillness

In the quiet moments, whispers pass,
Like secrets held within blades of grass.
The kettle sings a funny little tune,
While shadows dance beneath the moon.

I sat on a bench, my thoughts were wild,
Then a squirrel showed up, I felt like a child.
With acorns tucked, it looked so spry,
A lesson in joy, I began to pry.

A cup of tea, my wise little friend,
Shared tales of nonsense, they never end.
In stillness found a giggle or two,
A riddle unfolded, then a silly view.

As laughter bubbles, the world starts to spin,
I toss my troubles, let the fun begin.
Secrets in stillness, a treasure untold,
In each quiet giggle, gold turns to gold.

A Tapestry of Simple Truths

Threads of laughter woven in light,
Tangles of yarn in colors so bright.
A playful breeze tickles green leaves,
Waves of silliness, oh! how it weaves.

Chairs creak softly under the weight,
Of tales spun wildly, of quirky fate.
I spill my juice, it lands in a splash,
Who knew mishaps could be such a bash?

In every corner, a giggle resides,
Embracing the magic that silly confides.
A child drops ice cream, looks up and grins,
In those fleeting moments, true bliss begins.

With laughter's rhythm, we weave and bend,
A tapestry holding what we can mend.
In the simplest truths, we find our worth,
Fun binds us all, a dance on this earth.

The Radiance of a Clear Mind

Sunshine overhead, a clear sky blooms,
I chase after butterflies, then trip on fumes.
Each tiny blunder, a spark of delight,
With chuckles that echo, I take flight.

The toaster pops toast, it jumps to the stars,
While I pour my milk, and create bizarre bars.
Breakfast may falter, but spirits soar high,
With goofy mishaps, it's easy to try.

Dancing in puddles, splashes of glee,
Everyone's laughing, even the bee.
In a world of snickers, we share a soft sigh,
For in each moment, we learn to fly.

So embrace each blunder, let worries unwind,
For joy isn't lost, it's simply confined.
Radiance glows with a twinkle so bright,
In the playful shadows, we find our light.

A Dance in Gentle Breezes

In the park, I twirl around,
Chasing leaves that seek the ground.
A squirrel laughs, a branch does sway,
Who knew fun could come this way?

Cup of coffee spills with glee,
Drips like laughter down on me.
I leap and dodge, my steps a mess,
This chaos surely is a bless!

Stray dog joins, it's quite a sight,
We both just chase the morning light.
But as we dance, my shoe goes missing,
Was it my foot or the wind that's kissing?

The breeze, my partner, pulls me near,
I laugh aloud, I feel no fear.
Today I spin, tomorrow waltz,
How simple joy can be, no faults!

The Elegance of Everyday Moments

In the kitchen, I slice and chop,
Carrots fly, and onions plop.
A dance with utensils, I'm the star,
My dog's applause is from afar.

The clock ticks loud, my heart's in sync,
Spilling tea and forming links.
Salt and sugar waltz in cups,
I mix it all, but never fess up!

As clothes tumble, a sock takes flight,
Fuzzy whimsy, oh what a sight!
Who needs a plan, a scheme so grand?
I'll just let whimsy guide my hand.

With laughter echoing off the walls,
I trip through life and hear the calls.
Oh, elegance isn't so refined,
It's just the joy that you can find!

Finding Joy in the Mundane

On the bus, a toddler squeals,
His sandwich flies, oh what reveals!
A pigeon steals without a care,
Such antics hide in daily wear.

Laundry piles like mountains grow,
Where's that sock? Oh, now I know!
It's hiding beneath my cozy chair,
A treasure hunt, with laughs to spare.

Grocery lines, a waiting game,
Count the snacks, oh isn't it lame?
But there's a dance in scan and pay,
Like life's just a silly ballet.

In every chore, a flicker shines,
A quirk or laugh that intertwines.
Embrace the dull, the shine will beam,
For joy's the thread in every seam!

The Art of Uncomplicated Being

I forget my keys, I take a stroll,
Greet the flowers, that's my goal.
Each blossom grins without a care,
A simple truth floats in the air.

Dinner burns, smoke fills the room,
A culinary dance of doom!
But laughter reigns, I'll just order out,
Good food with friends, no room for doubt!

With mismatched socks, I strut with pride,
Colors clashing, nowhere to hide.
A running joke, a badge of fun,
In this everyday, I've clearly won.

So here's to joy in what we do,
To silly things and moments true.
Life's a canvas, bright and wide,
Paint it with laughter, let it slide!

Embracing the Easy Path

Woke up today with a grin,
Thought I might let silliness win.
Coffee spills, what a fine start,
Yet laughter spills into my heart.

Got lost in my own backyard,
But hey, it ain't that hard.
Chased a butterfly, took a dive,
Turns out I'm quite alive!

I tried to solve life's great puzzle,
But forgot where I put the huzzle.
Stumbling through like a clumsy fool,
Yet, oh, how I enjoy this school!

Let's dance like nobody's home,
In this world, we are free to roam.
Finding joy in little things,
In the chaos, laughter sings.

Heartbeats in Tranquil Spaces

In my garden, weeds grow high,
But who cares when birds fly by?
They sing and chirp, it's quite absurd,
A soothing sound, a gentle word.

My cat thinks he's chasing dreams,
Pawing shadows—are those the beams?
He naps while I ponder my plight,
Endless thoughts in the bright sunlight.

A breeze carries whispers so sweet,
Tickles my nose, can't stay on my feet.
For every worry, there's a giggle,
Here's to cuddles and the occasional wiggle!

In tranquil spaces, we find the key,
To laugh a little, be happy, be free.
The world spins on, and so do we,
All while sipping our cup of glee.

Lessons in Serene Existence

A snail meditates on the road,
While I rush with my heavy load.
What am I in such a fuss?
Serenity hides in the bus!

Pick up a stone, I find a geode,
A treasure's waiting, easily flowed.
Lessons come wrapped in silly ways,
Like dancing in puddles on rainy days.

The old man laughs—what a sight,
As he juggles apples in broad daylight.
With a wink, he shares his lore,
"Slow down, dear, there's so much more!"

I might just skip my grand plans,
And join in the game of silly jams.
For in stillness, the wisdom grows,
And life's a parade; who really knows?

Nature's Gentle Reminder

The flowers laugh, their petals sway,
While the sun beams down; it's a glorious day!
I trip on a root, and it's alright,
For even trees have their funny night.

Clouds drift lazily, puffs of cheer,
They whisper secrets for all to hear.
Why stress when the world holds its bliss?
Just hold my hand; let's dance like this.

Each leaf tells tales of joy and fun,
Even the mushrooms know how to run!
With every twist, this path unfolds,
Life's simple pleasures, treasures untold.

So let's toast to nature, our quirky guide,
With a wink and a laugh, we'll take it in stride.
For each silly moment we dare embrace,
Is a badge of honor in this zany race.

A Symphony of Baseline Happiness

In a world of hurried steps,
I sip my tea, let worries rest.
A sock that's lost, a laugh that swells,
In simplest joys, my heart now dwells.

I step on gum, it's stuck real tight,
Yet, here I stand with sheer delight.
The sun's a friend, it warms my face,
And life becomes a silly race.

My shoes are mismatched, oh what fun,
Dancing in puddles, I just run.
Each stumble's rhythm, each little fall,
Turns everyday woes into a ball.

So here's to joy, a symphony,
Playing the notes of ecstasy.
With laughter high, and stress laid low,
It's a dance of life, come join the show!

Scribbles of a Carefree Soul

I doodle hearts on napkin fade,
And laugh at plans that never made.
In chaos, find the sweetest thrill,
A topsy-turvy, chocolate spill.

The clock ticks on, its rhythm sly,
But I just grin and let time fly.
With every hiccup, giggle free,
I scribble joy, my own decree.

A cat that's perched on my old chair,
In sunshine's embrace, we share a stare.
Chasing shadows, both feel just right,
Life's a sketch, with colors bright.

So let the pen dance on the page,
As I embrace my silliness sage.
With every line, a tale unfolds,
It's all in fun, let joy be told!

Finding Clarity in Quiet Days

A lazy morn, no grand to-dos,
Just me and coffee, my favorite muse.
A squirrel debates on a tree branch high,
It twists and turns, just like my sighs.

The world can wait, it can unwind,
In silent moments, clarity I find.
With every sip, the noise does fade,
In gentle thoughts, a peace parade.

A jumbled sock drawer tells the tale,
Of mismatched adventures, without fail.
As daylight drifts in hues of gray,
I laugh at plans from yesterday.

So here I sit, in quiet bliss,
Embracing moments, that I can't miss.
In stillness I discover glee,
As life's soft whispers come to me.

The Freedom of Less

Juggling ten things, what a mess,
I throw them out; I feel so blessed.
With simpler choices, life's a breeze,
A break from chaos, oh sweet ease.

The clutter gone, my mind's a stream,
I dance to beats of a quiet dream.
Less to carry, more to play,
In this lightness, I find my way.

Old trinkets tossed, no strings attached,
Just humor left, and joy unmatched.
With open spaces, I twirl and spin,
In the freedom of less, I dive right in.

So let's declutter, let laughter reign,
In every moment, joy's the gain.
With each deep breath, I seize the zest,
In simplicity, I am truly blessed!

When Clarity Clicks

In the mirror I see my face,
Wondering about my place.
Should I bake or should I dance?
Why not both? Throw caution to chance!

I trip over socks like a pro,
Turns out my floor is a no-go.
A sandwich sitting on the shelf,
Me just laughing at my own self!

Those big questions swirling in my head,
Like what's for lunch, or is it bread?
I find the answers in my tea,
"Just relax!" whispered it to me.

A simple thought, I breathe in deep,
Why complicate? Just take a leap.
With a giggle, I wave goodbye,
To all the worries that just pass by.

The Dance of the Mundane

Dust bunnies dancing without a care,
As I sweep them, they leap in the air.
Each chore feels like a comedy show,
With the rhythm of a pro vacuum blow!

Coffee spills like an art piece rare,
I laugh at the chaos, if I dare.
Washing dishes, a soap bubble fight,
Maybe today isn't so uptight.

My laundry pile is a mountain high,
Yet I can't climb it, so I sigh.
Instead, I'll fashion a pillow fort,
And call my relaxation sport!

Juggling tasks with style and flair,
Maybe I'm just an expert at air.
Embracing the trivial, I found the sound,
Of silly joy, where I'm truly unbound.

Joy in the Shadows

In the corner, a shadow does nap,
The cat claims it; it's her own trap.
I trip over a misplaced shoe,
"Where's my other sock?" Who knows? Not you!

The fridge hums a little tune,
Chasing dreams like a cartoon.
An apple rolls like it's on a quest,
I'll join in; who needs to rest?

Glancing at my phone, trying to text,
Messages come back quite perplexed.
Misunderstandings lead to laughs,
And selfies with accidental giraffes!

In shadows, I find my hidden cheer,
Laughter echoes far and near.
In every misstep, there's glee to behold,
No treasure map—just stories untold.

Sipping Sunlight

Sunshine spills from my cup today,
Maybe I'm a plant? Who can say?
I'll bask in warmth with my cereal,
Munching through life, it tastes ethereal!

Birds chirp tunes I can't quite hum,
They're great at singing; I'm just numb.
The squirrel outside does acrobatics,
While I enjoy my own antics!

Days blend in with shades of fun,
Why overthink when I can run?
So cheers to random bursts of light,
And a whimsical outlook that feels just right!

With laughter as my guiding star,
I realize I'm never far,
From joy floating like a kite,
In simple moments, everything feels bright.

Reflections in a Calm Stream

In mirrors calm, I stare and see,
My odd reflections, wild and free.
A sock that's lost, a shoe askew,
I chuckle soft at what I view.

The ducks float by, no care at all,
While I just sit and start to sprawl.
With food on hand, and crumbs to spare,
The world spins round, I just sit there.

My thoughts are like those ripples small,
They dance with glee, then fade and fall.
What's serious? A mystery, true.
I'll just relax, how 'bout you?

In contemplation, I unwind,
The simplest joys are all I find.
Why run and rush, oh what a race!
I'll just enjoy this happy place.

In Praise of Simple Adventures

With spoon in hand, I take a dive,
Into the bowl where cereal thrives.
A chocolate milk mustache I wear,
What could be better? Nothing compares!

A trip to the fridge with daring flair,
I break a rule, I don't much care.
Leftover pizza, a bite or two,
Could there be snacks that stick like glue?

I stumble on socks that match not one,
Yet here I am, making it fun.
A dance in the kitchen, slapping my feet,
Each twirl a triumph, each spin a treat.

In every giggle, in every mess,
There's joy in finding happiness.
Let's celebrate these moments bright,
In playful ventures, pure delight.

Fragments of Joy

I tripped on air, oh what a sight,
The world just chuckled, oh so light.
With every fall, I laugh and bounce,
A dance among the crumbs, I flounce.

A cookie broken, but who would care?
I savor crumbs and giggle, "Fair!"
The dog looks up, his eyes a-glow,
As if he knows the treats will flow.

In every stumble, joy does sprout,
The silly times are what it's about.
We skip through puddles, shoes all wet,
A splash, a laugh, there's no regret.

So here's to shards of silly bliss,
In every moment, find a kiss.
Life is a puzzle tossed around,
In the chaos, joy is found.

The Softness of Unrushed Moments

Upon the couch, I sink so deep,
With snacks galore, it's time to creep.
A blanket fort is where I roam,
A treasure map that feels like home.

The clock's tick-tock becomes a friend,
It whispers soft, "There's time to spend."
Binge-watching shows, the world outside,
Just me and popcorn on this ride.

I chatter with my plants, so green,
They nod their leaves, so calm, serene.
No rush, no fuss, just cozy chats,
A life that's simple, full of laughs.

In quiet stillness, the world slows down,
I cherish moments without a frown.
Let's savor all the fun we find,
In softness shared, our hearts aligned.

Threads of Gratitude

I woke this day, socks don't match,
My coffee's cold, what a catch!
But with each sip, I give a grin,
Thankful for the chaos within.

My dog chews shoes, no sense of style,
Yet he makes me laugh, oh what a pile!
I trip on toys, I trip on crumbs,
Yet in this mess, my joy still hums.

A spider spun a web so grand,
While I untangle bread from my hand.
With every blunder, I learn to sway,
Grateful for messes that brighten my day.

In mismatched socks, a life I seek,
In silly moments, I feel unique.
Though things may tangle, I can't complain,
Each thread of gratitude is a silly gain.

Serenity in Simplicity

A meal so fine, it's just some toast,
With butter spread, I admire the ghost.
Of fancy dinners, that I could crave,
But burnt my bread? Oh well, I'm brave!

A garden grows, weeds in a show,
But daisies bloom, with joy they glow.
Between the chaos, there's laughter bright,
In simple pleasures, all feels right.

My cat naps hard, by the sunny beam,
While I chase thoughts, not quite a dream.
Yet even in naps, wisdom unfolds,
In simple ways, serenity holds.

So here I stand, with crumbs in my lap,
Finding joy in my silly mishaps.
For in each moment, there's grace to find,
In simplicity, peace of mind.

Relaxing into Routine

Each morning starts with a dance of socks,
And tripping over my garden rocks.
Toast pops up, smoke in the air,
Yet the fragrance is bliss, I don't despair.

The news blares loud, a circus of yore,
While I sip tea and soon hit the floor.
A routine forms and then gets bent,
Yet I giggle at where the time went.

The dishes stack, a mountain-like feat,
I ask my dog, 'Why are we beat?'
He wags and rolls, as if to say,
That messy corners are here to stay.

So here's to routines, a wobbly chase,
With giggles and grumbles, we find our place.
For in this whirlwind, there's peace to glean,
In the bounds of madness, a day serene.

The Canvas of Calm

Oh crayons scattered across the floor,
While I pretend to be quite the chore.
Paint splatters dance, oh what a sight,
My masterpiece? A mess, but it feels right!

Life unfolds like a canvas wide,
With smudges and blurs, where dreams can hide.
I laugh at my brush, what a clumsy stroke,
Yet every mistake's a new laugh, a joke.

When colors clash, I see the fun,
In every mishap, I find the sun.
So I'll paint away with silly glee,
Creating a world that's just for me.

In a sea of calm, I splash and play,
Finding treasures in each silly fray.
For art may mess, but joy will bloom,
In the chaos where I find my room.

Sunlight Filtering Through the Clouds

Woke up today, jumped out of bed,
My coffee machine laughed, filled my head.
The socks mismatched, a fashion faux pas,
But who really cares? I'm my own star!

The world spins fast, yet here I stand,
Tripping on life, yet feeling so grand.
A pigeon coos, as if to say,
Just enjoy the ride, come what may!

Clouds may loom, but I see the sun,
Skinned my knee, but I still had fun.
The grass is green, the sky's azure,
Turns out my worries are quite obscure!

Giggles echo through streets and lanes,
I dance like no one sees the stains.
So here's to days, so often bright,
Finding joy in silly, things done right!

Breath of Fresh Perspectives

Out in the park, I grab a snack,
My lunch flies off! Oh, what a whack!
Squirrels join in, a cheeky feast,
Who knew chaos could bring such at least?

A dog in shades sauntered by,
His owner grumbled, "Oh my, oh my!"
Can't help but smile, life's little jest,
Always means to put humor to the test.

Each twist and turn invites a laugh,
Like stepping on a bubble wrap path.
Today I'll dance, twirl with delight,
Laughing even when things aren't quite right!

With every breath, I find new cheer,
Embrace the silly, lose the fear.
For fresh perspectives bring with ease,
A tickle of joy, a moment to please!

Navigating with Laughter

Maps in my pocket? Nah, I'm more chill,
Following ducks, it's a quirky thrill.
When the GPS bounces, I just grin wide,
What's lost is now just a fun little ride!

A seagull squawks, steals my sandwich joy,
But I laugh it off – just a winged ploy.
Get lost in giggles, misstep and roll,
Turns out my journey is the ultimate goal.

Every twist here, looks like a dance,
I spin and frolic, give life a chance.
Roads aren't straight, but oh how they bend,
With laughter as fuel, the trip won't end!

So grab a hat, put on the fun,
Navigating boldly, I'm never done.
With silly detours, I'm always amazed,
At how much laughter leaves me praised!

Clear Waters, Reflecting Truth

Staring at the pond, it's not so deep,
I tossed a pebble, watch the ripples leap.
Nature giggles, shows me the way,
"Keep it simple!" it seems to say.

The ducks quack loud, they have no care,
Waddling by, they strut and stare.
In mirrored waters, truth does appear,
Be like the ducks, have no fear!

Sunshine dances on each little wave,
A reminder that fun is what we crave.
Deep thoughts are great, but don't dive too hard,
Stick to the surface; it's not that scarred!

With each reflection, I chuckle and smile,
Life's just a game; make it worthwhile.
So splash about, let go of that strife,
In clear waters, we find our real life!

A Smile Among the Stones

A rock sat still, observing me,
I asked it why it wouldn't flee.
It chuckled back, a gravelly tone,
"Why rush, dear friend? I'm just a stone."

I tripped and fell, then burst with glee,
The grass just laughed, said, "Look at thee!"
A tumble here is just a dance,
With every fall, there's a silly chance.

The sun rolled in, a cheerful glow,
Said, "Why so serious? Let's take it slow!"
With daisies swaying, all took part,
In a funny waltz, a giggling heart.

So here's the truth, wrapped in jest,
A laid-back world is more than best.
With each small joy, hear nature's tones,
A hearty laugh among the stones.

Laughter's Unseen Path

I wandered down a winding way,
Where shadows danced and children play.
The road was crooked, signs askew,
Yet joy arrived, as if it knew.

A squirrel paused, its cheeks were round,
It chattered loud, such silly sound!
I joined its game, we laughed a while,
Both thieves of time, in mischief's style.

Oh, the trees had secrets, wise and grand,
Giggling leaves, a jolly band.
Each step unfolded frolicsome sights,
With whimsies growing in fuzzy tights.

In giggles found, I walked with ease,
Chasing wonders, like a breeze.
For laughter leads where joy imparts,
A sunny seat in wandering hearts.

Nature's Whisper in Every Breath

A butterfly grinned, with wings so wide,
Flitting by with a splendid glide.
I asked it, "How do you know to be?"
It winked then said, "It's light, you see!"

Clouds puffed joy in a cotton ball,
"Float along, you won't trip or fall!"
I chatted with daisies, so fresh and bright,
They told me to dance in morning light.

The river giggled, splashing fun,
Said, "Worry not, we'll always run."
I felt its rhythm, a carefree beat,
With every ripple, my fears retreat.

In nature's voice, the laughter grows,
A symphony only the heart knows.
Breathe it in; oh, catch that breath,
For joy resides in every depth.

Threads of Ease

I sewed my troubles with threads of cheer,
Stitched them close, spun laughter near.
Each knot a story, each loop a rhyme,
In every stitch, I found more time.

Pulling on fabric made from glee,
My worries faded, oh can't you see?
The bobbin laughed with every spin,
While clothes danced lightly in the wind.

Unraveled tales of silly plight,
A t-shirt claimed to be my knight.
It wore a smile, so wide and bright,
With every thread, I took to flight.

In this patchwork world of friendly seams,
I found the magic in simple dreams.
So let's all weave with playful ease,
For laughter's fabric is sure to please.

Building Castles from Clouds

I tried to build a castle in the air,
With pillow stones and a blanket fair.
Yet as I stood proud, it floated away,
Guess dreams are slippery, what can I say?

My towers of fluff, were a sight so grand,
But the wind had plans I didn't understand.
I laughed as I chased my imaginary throne,
Turns out I'm just a king of my own home.

When friends joined me for a wild cloud fight,
We knocked down the turrets, but what a sight!
With giggles and whimsy, we fluffed up the sky,
Who needs foundations? Just let laughter fly!

At the end of the day, in our scattered dreams,
We learned castles are built on laughter it seems.
So here's to the clouds, and our folly-filled jest,
In the kingdom of fun, we are truly blessed!

The Lightness of Being Present

I woke up this morning, no plans in my head,
Just coffee and laughter, that's how to be fed.
I tripped over socks, what a glorious fall,
Yet here I am smiling, living it all!

A bird stole my muffin right off my table,
Noticing little things makes me more stable.
A breeze rolled by, blowing feathers anew,
Who needs a schedule when all I need is a view?

The cat made a jump, a spectacular flop,
As I giggle and watch, I just can't stop.
The world spins on whimsies, I'm dancing along,
What's life without humor and a silly song?

If being present brings more joy than a plan,
I'll embrace every moment, oh yes, I can!
With laughter as my compass, wherever I roam,
I'll always find lightness to guide me back home!

Comfort in Familiar Places

There's magic in routine, it's a cozy old chair,
Where I sip my tea with a cinnamon flair.
My favorite old sweater, worn and slightly torn,
Wraps me in warmth like a hug from the dawn.

At the corner café with the sticky old floor,
They know my order; it's a comfort galore.
The same waiter winks as he brings me my mug,
In this familiar world, I can truly unplug.

The park where I wander, my laughter the tune,
Where the ducks all quack in a funny commune.
I toss them some crumbs; they dance and they twirl,
In the comfort of company, my heart starts to swirl.

So here's to the places that feel like a hug,
In the simplest corners, I find my warm snug.
Life may be wild, but in places I know,
The laughter and comfort will always help me grow!

Petals on a Still Pond

Petals drift gently on a mirror so sly,
Like thoughts on my mind, just floating by.
I've tried to catch them, but they twirl and sway,
To grab life too tightly? Oh, that's not my way!

The frog on a lily plays banjo with glee,
Croaking out rhythms just for me.
While I sit and ponder my grand master plan,
He looks at me oddly, with a smile so grand.

What if the secret is simply to float?
To ride every wave, let them capsize my boat?
With each petal that dances, I giggle and spin,
Maybe chaos is where the fun must begin!

So here's to the moments that make us all pause,
Like petals on water, we find our own cause.
Life's random splashes can bring a big grin,
With laughter and petals, let the madness begin!

In the Shade of Unseen Joys

Underneath the sunny skies,
I lost my keys, what a surprise!
But in the grass, I found a shoe,
And pondered how that might be you.

A squirrel danced with such delight,
Stealing snacks, then took off in flight.
I chuckled loud, forgot my plight,
And waved goodbye with all my might.

In puddles deep, reflections play,
A skipping stone, I start to sway.
With every splash, my worries fade,
While ants prepare their grand parade.

So here I sit, just soaking sun,
Life's little whims are so much fun.
Between the laughs and silly games,
Who knew the joy of silly names?

A Canvas of Simple Dreams

I painted clouds in shades of cheese,
With honey bees that hum and tease.
A canvas stretched with laughter bright,
Where silly thoughts take to the flight.

In this art, I find a cat,
That wears a hat and loves to chat.
He tells me tales of sockless feet,
With every giggle, feels so sweet.

A cupcake sky with sprinkles rains,
While bouncing jellybeans make gains.
The colors swirl, the brushes dance,
Each stroke a wink, a silly chance.

So let's create, with joy unfurled,
A world that makes the heart feel swirled.
With every laugh, a color gleams,
In our bizarre, delightful dreams.

The Laughter of Little Things

A feather floats, a tickle breeze,
Inviting giggles cascades with ease.
A tiny bug wears shades so cool,
And struts like royalty, oh what a fool!

The sunbeams dance upon my nose,
While grasshoppers compose their prose.
Each hop a burst of blissful cheer,
Reminding me that fun is near.

With cookies baked in shapes of stars,
And sprinkles bright, like little cars.
I munch and grin, the day's a play,
A charm that's sweet in every way.

So join the fun, let worries slide,
In giggles shared, our hearts collide.
For every smile, a joy that sings,
The world comes alive with little things.

Moments Like Soft Petals

In gardens where the daisies sway,
I tripped and found a charming way.
A tumble here, a laugh out loud,
Chasing dreams, I feel so proud.

The butterfly wore stripes of glee,
A curious friend who danced with me.
We twirled in circles, soft and free,
In a world that's sweet as sugar tea.

Each petal whispering sweet surprise,
As I caught glimpses, in the skies.
The vending machine ate my dime,
But laughter fills the air with rhyme.

So take a chance, and let it show,
The joy of moments, let it grow.
In every chuckle, every sigh,
There's peace and magic, flying high.

Echoes of Laughter in Still Waters

In a world so vast and wide,
Who knew I'd trip on a shoe tie?
Chasing dreams like a frantic dance,
I stumbled once, oh what a chance!

A cat on a roof, meows with glee,
While I search for my cup of tea.
Surfing on waves of sock and mud,
Just a giggle in the midst of the flood.

Riding bikes with a wobbly grin,
Fell in the flowers, oh where to begin?
The bees buzz around, in sweet delight,
Humorous chaos, life feels just right.

And when I think of that silly past,
I smile at moments, too quick to last.
Echoes of laughter, like a soft breeze,
Make the journey a breeze, oh so easy!

When Time Stood Still

Once I tried to bake a pie,
Forgot the sugar—oh my, oh my!
The kitchen looked like a flour bomb,
Time stopped as I tried to stay calm.

Waiting for toast while it chose to burn,
I pondered if I'd ever learn.
A laugh with my dog, as he gave me a stare,
"Who needs a chef? You're beyond compare!"

Clock hands tangled in silly fights,
Hours lost in board game nights.
When time stood still in a laughing spree,
Every moment was just wild and free.

Chasing shadows on a sunny floor,
I tripped on laughter, fell once more.
With friends by my side, we danced with zest,
In these simple joys, I found my quest.

The Heart's Gentle Compass

With a heart that giggles while it spins,
Navigating chaos, where fun begins.
A compass that points to ticklish dreams,
In the silliest moments, laughter redeems.

Searching for socks that wander alone,
A treasure hunt in my cluttered home.
The heart chuckles at the mess we make,
Finding joy in each funny mistake.

Maps of giggles leading the way,
Through the blunders of an ordinary day.
"Oops, that's not coffee but orange juice!"
In the simple mix-ups, I claim my truce.

And so I chart my playful course,
With chuckles and smiles that spring forth.
The heart's gentle compass knows no bounds,
In the journey of joy, pure laughter resounds!

Celebrating the Ordinary Journey

Balancing dishes like it's a sport,
Who knew chaos could jump and cavort?
In socks that don't match, I strut with pride,
This ordinary journey, what a wild ride!

Mundane errands filled with jest,
Grocery lists that I often guessed.
Forgotten veggies lead me to laugh,
On this quirky, delightful path!

Picnics on blankets with food piled high,
Seagulls swoop down like they're sky-high.
A sandwich flies off, what a funny sight,
We dance with the wind, all day and night!

So here's to days that seem quite plain,
Where giggles poke through like sun through rain.
Celebrating the ordinary, come what may,
In this hilarious journey, we joyfully play!

Unmasking the Ordinary

I woke up this morning, the sun shining bright,
Tripped on my shoelace, oh what a sight!
Coffee on my shirt, a little stain,
Yet, I wore it proudly, chaos my gain.

The cat's got my toast, and it looks so smug,
House full of clutter, yet I still feel snug.
Called up a friend, we laughed till we cried,
In simple moments, my worries subside.

Life's not a puzzle, just pieces that play,
Like socks in the dryer, they vanish away.
I chased down my dreams, but they ran quite fast,
So I joined the parade, and had a blast!

Now I dance with my shadows, twirl with the breeze,
In a world of confusion, I're found my ease.
Let's toast to the silly, the hilariously grand,
For ordinary wonders are close at hand.

Echoes of a Peaceful Mind

Woke up this morning, what time is it?
I chased my own tail, oh isn't that neat?
Coffee's brewing chaos, but I'm feeling fine,
Sat down to ponder, where's that lost wine?

Thoughts dance like butterflies, flitting about,
One moment a worry, the next, a shout.
Messy hair and pajamas, oh what a sight,
Yet, I twirl around, with all of my might.

Naps can be tricky, they steal such time,
But a slice of cake brings back the sublime.
So I binge on the random, embrace the spree,
With laughter and snacks, it's just fancy glee!

Why fret about deadlines, or bills piling high?
I'll serenade squirrels as they scurry by.
To live in the moment, without any bind,
Is the riddle I ponder, a peaceful mind.

The Gentle Art of Being

In the garden of chaos, I tend to my weeds,
A flower blooms bright, but so do the seeds.
Wiggling my toes in the warm summer grass,
As I fumble with daisies, oh, how they sass!

I tried yoga once, fell flat on my face,
But laughter erupted and filled up the space.
With each pose a giggle, I found my own flow,
Turns out being clumsy is how I let go!

Chasing my shadow, let me be free,
The sun makes my heart sing, just wait and see.
With cake on my cheek, I skip on a whim,
In the art of just being, I feel so trim!

So here's to the flops, the stumbles, the fun,
In the dance of discomfort, I've finally won.
For in every misstep, there's joy to behold,
In the gentle art of just being, I'm bold.

Savoring the Small Wins

Got out of bed? That's a win for today!
The sun winked at me, said, 'Come out and play!'
Toasted my breakfast, forgot the jam,
Still grinning like I found a rare clover sham.

Counted my blessings, just one, two, three,
Turns out I have more than a boat full of glee.
Each sock that I match feels like such a feat,
In the grand scheme of things, it's a tasty treat.

Slipped on my flip-flops, they're maroon and bright,
Took a stroll outside, what a marvelous sight!
Puddles to jump, oh isn't it grand?
With each tiny victory, I wave my hand.

So let's raise a toast to the moments we gain,
To the chocolate that melts, and the joy in the rain.
For in savoring small wins, we find the delight,
And in funny missteps, the world feels just right.

www.ingramcontent.com/pod-product-compliance
Lightning Source LLC
Chambersburg PA
CBHW051650160426
43209CB00004B/859